I'm Not God, I'm Just a Woman

By
Evangelist Shevelle Ford

I'M NOT GOD, I'M JUST A WOMAN

To contact the author:

A.J. Ford Ministries
P.O. Box 86061
Baton Rouge, LA 70879
1-866-HIGHER-G (866-444-4374)

mrsjaford@aol.com

ISBN:978-0-9779572-0-0

Printed in the United States of America
Copyright © 2006 by Evangelist Shevelle Ford

Red Sea Productions
P.O. Box 86028
Baton Rouge, LA 70879

American Press, Inc.
12527 South Choctaw Drive
Baton Rouge, LA 70815
Phone: 225-275-7831 • www.CallAmericanPress.com

All rights reserved. No part of this book may be reproduced in any form, except for the inclusion of brief quotations in a review, without permission in writing from the author or publisher.

In Memory of My Daddy

The late Rev. Dr. Percy Murphy Griffin
The Gentle Giant

I miss you so much!!

To My Husband

Words cannot express how grateful I am to God for joining us together. I was your choice and a good one I might add. Without you this project would not have been possible. Over the years you have managed to pull things out of me that I didn't even know were there. You've midwifed the birth of many gifts and talents, at the same time, allowing me to be free to be who God created me to be. You are my **engine-engine number nine** and the wind beneath my wings. It amazes me that after eleven years of marriage, two kids, a business and a full-time ministry, you still manage to make me laugh. So many people lack the joy of laughter in their lives, having lost sight of the simple things in life. I thank God for keeping us grounded. Thank you so much for releasing me and allowing your mantle to rest on my life. You are my husband. You are the head of this marriage, and I submit to your authority. Beyond all of that, you are my friend. I love you so much. Guess what sweetheart? Effective immediately, Mr. Toshiba (my laptop) is out of our bed for a little while.

Keep loving me,
Your wife

Acknowledgements

First and foremost I thank God for choosing me, you didn't have to do it, but I'm glad you did.

A special thanks to my Nubian Queen, my mom Irene. You're the best. Without you and dad I would not be here today.

I am so thankful to all of my siblings: Murphy, Percy V., Roland, Rommel, Dexter, Quintin, James, Geessler, and Tracey, for all of your love and support throughout my entire life.

Hugs and kisses to Trinity and AJ for their laughter and encouragement, through the years. Guess what guys? Yep, mommy's book is finally done.

Thank you, thank you, thank you, to my longtime friend and editor, Tia Landry Alexander.

Lots of love to my other big sister, Judith Sonnier, for your help and support.

I dare not forget to thank Ms. Alma Molix for her sound judgement, keen wisdom, and wonderful personality.

Much gratitude and appreciation to Higher Grounds International Worship Center and AJ Ford Ministries, especially our wonderful full-time staff: Roderick, Tyra, Meka, Tim, Belinda, Lee, Salunda, Danielle, Adrian and Calvin. Keep up the good work!

I will never forget the late Dr. Yvonne Ochillo, an instructor at Dillard University, who saw a gift in me to write years ago.

In the past year I've lost two special people in my life, my mother-in-law, Lucille Spland, and my father-in-law, the Rev. Robert Ford, you are both sadly missed.

Every writer should have a book committee like mine; you guys are a God-send.

Thanks a bunch to Mr. Pete DiBenidetto at American Press for your flexibility.

And lastly, to Red Sea Productions, we did it!

Forward

I believe one of the greatest gifts God has given to the crown of His creation man, is the gift of potential. Potential is the ability to achieve or become something in the future. Unfortunately, potential is one of the gifts least discovered by the human race. Even more disheartening, of the few who do tap into this precious gift, oftentimes releases it in a negative, selfish and or wicked way.

Fortunately for us, Shevelle not only discovered this gift, but embraced its power. Believing in its presence, she has elected to release it upon the world. Stripping herself of her personal ambitions and choosing courage over her own inhibitions, she charts a course to freedom for those who are entangled in the snares of this life. This new young author emerges from the matrix of dormancy, on a crusade for social liberation. Freedom always comes with a price, so I thank God for Shevelle, who is willing to share the spoils of her warfare.

The word of God teaches that ye shall know the truth and the truth shall make you free. This book is not only entertaining, but edifying and enlightening. Each chapter of the book contains a touch of revelation knowledge, as well as practical everyday scenarios that will allow the reader to see herself plastered within its pages. Chapter after chapter strips away the life diminishing mental adhesives, which entrap us into social bondages.

Prepare your mind for a thrill ride; loops of laughter, turns of tears, and elevations of enlightenment. And when the ride is all over, and you disembark from the final page of the book, you will feel the freedom to acknowledge, *"I'm not God, I'm Just a Woman."*

Bishop Joseph (AJ) Ford
AJ Ford Ministries
Baton Rouge, LA.

Table of Contents

Introduction 1

Created in the Image 7

I am Anointed To Do What I Do 15

Enjoy the State the Lord Has Called You To 23

Don't Let People Put You In a Box 35

Just Because You're Invited, Doesn't Mean You Have to Go .. 51

I'm Too Tired 61

Finally 73

Introduction

So many times in life as women we find ourselves wearing many different hats, playing many different roles, quite often at the same time. In the midst of being mother, wife, sister, confidant, cheerleader, housekeeper, errand-girl, teacher, nurse and whomever or whatever our loved ones need us to be, we have a tendency to lose touch with who we are. Nearly eight years ago God gave me a revelation of how much responsibility rest in the care of a woman. It was a mind-blowing experience that happened one Sunday evening; actually it was the day after I preached my first sermon. I was lying on the sofa, enjoying the luxury of a quiet moment, when out of nowhere everyone started screaming for my attention. My daughter Trinity wanted something to eat, my son A.J. wanted to nurse, my husband was calling me for something, and my mother-in-law was knocking at the door. Feeling so overwhelmed, not being able to decide who needed me the most or what to do first, I began to yell, "I'm not God, I'm just a woman!" Then in a very meek almost defeated voice, out of my mouth I could hear these words, "I can't be everything to everyone at the same time." For a moment it seemed liked the whole world stopped spinning. They all looked at me as if to say, she can't be serious, she'll be whatever we want her to be. Recognizing that those vultures were not about to have any sympathy for my moment I got myself together and did what was needed.

Later that night God began to tell me, "Yes, you are just a

woman; you are neither omnipresent nor omnipotent." He reminded me that I was created in the image and that I wasn't the image. Ultimately, He shared the importance of me needing to know how to prioritize my life. Enlightend to the fact that I was not a lone ranger and that so many women felt the same way I did, overworked and underpaid. Always having too many irons in the fire and always attempting to master the juggling act just to make it through the day. He gave me an assignment that night to write this book, but my body was drained both mentally and physically. I was very disobedient, because I didn't have the energy to obey Him. I felt like Peter, James, and John when they were in the Garden of Gethsemane and Jesus asked them to watch for Him just one hour. (Matthew 26:36-42) Their spirit was willing but their flesh was, just as I was, weak. Several weeks after that night, He would wake me up very early in the morning, and I could feel His Anointing present in the room for me to write, but my flesh was in control. I would just lie in my bed and wrestle with only the desire to do God's will. After many sleepless nights, I decided to put forth an effort. Getting up with pen and paper in hand, I remember telling God, "Okay, here I am, tell me what you will have me to write, in my quest to help my sisters out," but He would not say a word, dead silence. Ain't it funny when we decide to obey God, we act as if we're doing Him a favor. We have a tendency to forget that we need Him to continue

Introduction

to speak life and direction that we may continue to walk in His perfect will for our lives. Ignoring the fact that God was not speaking, I decided to get started anyway. I jotted down some ideas of what I thought this book should be about, and believe me when I say that they were my ideas, not His (God's). Finally, I reached a point where I was so frustrated because I couldn't sleep; as a result I was always irritable. I could hear these thoughts in my head constantly, but was unable to transpose them to paper. Knowing that I couldn't go on living like that and realizing that something had to give, I attempted to do what some refer to as, "Calling God on The Carpet." Yes, I began to have a little talk with my "Daddy," or should I say a monologue because I was the only one talking. I pleaded with Him for another chance to say yes to His will for my life; reminding Him that He knew better than I, all that I had to do. **My plate was full!** He had just given me a vision to start a business, my husband had just started pastoring a little Baptist church, and I had to be his biggest, and in most cases, his only cheerleader. I had two kids that were 20 months apart and had no family near me for support. My mom and dad lived over two and a half hours away and my father was very ill, so I would travel home weekly to help care for him. As if all of that wasn't enough, I had just accepted the call to preach the Gospel of Jesus Christ. I had no experience in writing; let the truth be told, other than the word of God, I hated reading. My list went on and on because you can do that on "the carpet." That is your opportunity to lay it all on the line. I must admit that my God is truly a gentleman, not once did He interrupt me. He allowed me the opportunity to get everything off my chest and still did not speak anything different than what He told me at first, "you need to prioritize your life." For some reason I expected Him to say something different, maybe it was just me. But I had just had a tantrum (eyes swollen, nose running, head hurting, the works) and I wanted to hear; "daughter I understand," "it's going to be okay," "don't worry about it," "we'll try later," but not my God, the exact word He had given me before is what He spoke again. I promise you it was as if something phenomenal happened that very instant, the word was the same but I was different. The switch was turned on, my eyes were opened, and I was able to see, for the first time, how hectic my life was, and realized the true need for some sort of order. I must admit that it was a little overwhelming to see all that God had entrusted me with. God showed me why so many of His daughters are so frustrated and what I could do to help them. I saw how vital a role the woman plays in the success or failure of her family. Having many hats to wear and roles to play, we have to know how to balance our lives, so that in the midst of everything, we are able to effectively do our part in keeping it all together. Understanding now, that it's not up to me to keep the

Introduction

whole thing together. I have a part to play and it is imperative to my sanity that I understand my role and do it without hesitation of the next person's position.

I tapped into the spiritual realm for wisdom and direction on how to handle what seemed to me to be an impossible task. Organization was never one of my strong points. I am a true procrastinator, always waiting until the last minute to do everything. For years I thought I worked better under pressure. I had no notion of how to prioritize my day not to mention the rest of my life. But God is good, and his mercy endures forever. There is hope. God, having no respect of person, stepped into my life and in the midst of the storm declared, "peace be still." He did it for me and He wants to do it for you. As you continue to read this book, pray that God will open your eyes that you can see YOU. My daily prayer is "God, show me, me, not my husband or those around me, I want to see what I can do to make my situation better." My prayer for you is that this book will enhance your relationship with God and that you will gain insight on how to prioritize your life in your quest to fulfill His perfect will for you. Keep in mind that, *I'm Not God, I'm Just a Woman.*

I'm Not God, I'm Just a Woman

CHAPTER ONE
CREATED IN THE IMAGE

So God created man in His own image, in the image of God created He him; male and female created He them.
—*Genesis 1:27 NKJV*

We are created in the image; we are not the image. A man created with a womb. There are some characteristics about a woman that are irrelevant to race or creed. Our bodies are designed to incubate and reproduce. It is our basic instinct to nurture and care. A woman can be as gentle as a dove and without notice can become as fierce as a bear when her cubs are in danger.

One of our biggest dilemmas is our inability to recognize our own limitations. Too often we find ourselves attempting to play God in people's lives. We want to love and care for everyone, which creates a problem when we begin to lend our time, attention, and energy to people that do not need it or even worse do not want it. Even when our feelings get hurt and we find ourselves being used and abused; something inside still tells us to love. We are emotional creatures and most decisions we make are based on our emotions. Logic is normally not a part of the plan. Frequently torn between what our heart wants verses what our mind and body needs, relentlessly leads us to emotional turmoil. Some of us waste years of our precious time carrying people and things that we have no business carrying, and dealing with issues that in all actuality, we have no business dealing with.

In our effort to help, oftentimes we actually end up hurting and crippling the very thing we intended to nurture. A lot of us feel like we are trapped and will find ways to justify our irrational behavior to ourselves and others. Constantly operating in the Red Zone and not even recognizing it. We are like walking time bombs waiting to explode because of the toxins that we are carrying. If we are not careful our quest to help others will result in our own demise, so watch out for the Red Zone! That place where all are advised to proceed with caution.

The Bible gives an excellent illustration that I use as a measuring tool to let me know when I'm out of my zone and creeping into the Red Zone. Luke 1:39-41 talks about what happened when Mary was pregnant with Jesus and she walked into the house and greeted her cousin Elizabeth. The writer records that the thing that Elizabeth was carrying leaped and she was filled with the Holy Ghost. Not with pain, frustration, or anger, but a gift from God. After reading that passage of scripture I began to do a quick evaluation. I needed to know what type of stuff I was carrying and what was it filling my life with. Because the truth of the matter is that it cost to carry people in the spirit and in the natural. Elizabeth carried John the Baptist and when the baby leaped, her life was changed forever.

Created in the Image

As a rule of thumb, if the thing that I'm lending my attention to is not benefiting me, yet on the contrary is hurting me, then there is a problem. If it causes my mood to change in a negative swing every time it presents itself, something is wrong. If the mere thought causes the hairs on the back of my neck to rise, that lets me know that I am definitely out of my zone. When these things begin to happen I know beyond a shadow of a doubt, that I'm attempting to handle something that was not designed for me (the created image) to handle. If the prenatal vitamins (the word of God) taken daily as prescribed, is of no effect and I always feel tired and drained, something has to give. Because if I'm not able to be nourished properly, the thing that I'm carrying will suck the life out of me and I will die.

When I was pregnant with my son A.J., I remember going to one of my prenatal visits and discussing with my doctor how taxing that pregnancy was compared to my first pregnancy. He questioned me about my eating habits and wanted to make sure that I was taking my prenatal vitamins daily. Admitting that I would skip a few here and there made him a little annoyed at me. He explained to me that most people have a misconception of who the prenatal vitamins are really for. To my surprise, I learned that the vitamins were for my benefit and not the baby's. The baby is going to get everything it needs, even if it has to drain the mother in the process.

I'm Not God, I'm Just a Woman

Because of all that we do, it is necessary that we draw strength from the word of God. In our daily walk we encounter circumstances and situations that if we're not careful, they will destroy us. Think about it, we lose weight, have anxiety attacks, and have many sleepless nights in our efforts to save our world. The word of God refers to us as being the weaker vessel, and in many aspects we are, but I find it unique that a creature can be so timid and frail yet possess the strength to maintain a stable environment. If you think it's not true, get sick for a week and see what happens to your family. I once saw a commercial on TV when the wife caught the flu and the house went to hell. Why? Because nine times out of ten, the responsibility of the family rests upon the woman.

It is important for us to establish boundaries and guidelines to what we lend our time and attention to. Many times we become immune to situations that should be foreign. We have to recognize that we are created in the image; we cannot allow the enemy to make us think that we are the image. Accept the fact that you are human and that you have limitations, it's a part of life. We have to stop allowing the devil to run rampant in our lives. **Choose your battles.** No matter how many times a package is shipped to your address, if you don't want it, you can write a note that says, "return to sender." And hear me when I say that some stuff the devil sends should be sent back stamped "address unknown." The enemy tries to impregnate us with spirits of low self-esteem, anger, defeat, desire to quit, and all sorts of craziness, when in all actuality the devil cannot give life; therefore, anything he releases into our lives is designed to kill and destroy us. I've learned that the antidote to the enemy's attack is finding God's will for your life. Stop trying to be Superwoman, wanting people to think that you can do it all and getting upset when their expectations become unrealistic. It's time to remove the mask and be real with yourself and others around you. I don't know about anyone else but I get tired of the juggling act, but don't know what to let go of. It always seems like just when I have the routine mastered, something else is added to the equation and the frustration starts all over again. Sometimes I want to yell, "HELP! I need a break." I need a breakthrough before I breakout. Yes, there are times when I want to quit. Questioning whether or not I may have missed God, concerning this path for my life. I get tired of the pull and long for an impartation. Having so many people that depend on me, yet feeling like I have no one that I can depend on.

Not long ago I reached a point in my marriage when I felt like I had no one to talk to. Not good. I couldn't talk to my pastor because he was my husband. I tried role playing with him once before and that was a waste of time. I didn't have any pastor friends that I felt comfortable with, because one thing I've learned about people is that they will take one incident and attempt to use it as a measuring tool for the rest of your life. I didn't know if the problem was serious enough for me to go to our father in the ministry, so I said the heck with it, regrouped, and pressed my way. Because the reality is that we can't give up now. My husband tells me all the time that if I should ever leave him to make sure I pack him a bag because he's going to leave him too. In other words, no matter what, we've committed to making this thing work. When we first got married, we would always say that we refuse to be together if we're not happy. After going through years of stuff that made us both unhappy, we changed our confession to whatever it takes to make our marriage a happy one, we'll do it.

It blows my mind when people quit the race in the last lap. What's the logic? If you are going to quit, do it around the second lap. If you must, count up the cost and if you're not able to trust God for what you don't see, then leave it alone.

I recently started working out and a personal goal that I've set for myself is to run three miles on the treadmill. There are days when I get to the last mile and my body begins to send signals to my brain to let it know that it's tired and it wants to stop. At that moment my mind takes control over my body and I begin to encourage myself. In other words, why wait until the kids finish high school and then get divorced? Why quit school your last semester?

Created in the Image

If you've made it this far, why not believe God to see you through. Let the truth be told, all of us have taken more stuff than we thought we could take and have gone farther than we thought we could go. When we begin to recognize the force that's behind us, we'll give Him (God) the glory and keep pressing on. **IT'S TIME TO LET GOD BE GOD!**

I'm Not God, I'm Just a Woman

CHAPTER TWO
I AM ANOINTED TO DO WHAT I DO

Thou preparest a table before me in the presence of mine enemies: thou anointest my head with oil, my cup runneth over.
—*Psalms 23:5KJV*

For years I would scream, "My plate is full, not today maybe tomorrow," was normally after good morning. For the life of me I could not figure it out, always feeling like I was stretched to the max and before long something else would be added to my agenda. Grasping an understanding from the word of God, that He would never put any more on me than I'm able to bear and believing that the Word is true, compelled me to take a closer look at what was really going on. Looking at the real picture allowed me to see that there was a force greater than I that enabled me to keep my sanity. Honestly, when I look back over my life, it wasn't me. There are events in my memory bank that I am oblivious as to how I made it through. I could really see the illustration of the poem that I read years ago when I was a little girl entitled, "Footprints." In the poem the writer reflects over his life and notes that throughout his life he was able to see two sets of footprints in the sand, one belonging to him and the other to God. But one thing that puzzled him and he questioned God about, was that every time it seemed like he had trouble in his life he only noticed one set of footprints and wanted to know why? God explained to him that it was through those tough times that He carried him. And just like that writer there have been times in my life that God had to carry me.

People would ask me all the time, "How do you do it?" Do what? As far as I was concerned, I was just attempting to make it happen. Until I started meeting people whose lives were parallel to mine in a sense, but they suffered from hypertension, anxiety, some had strokes, nervous break downs, heart attacks, you name it. I'm not exaggerating, as a pharmacist, I've encountered many patients that would take a pill to get up out of bed in the morning and take another pill to go to sleep at night. One day the thought crossed my mind that if we had any idea of how medicated our co-workers, friends, family members, and the driver in the next lane was over ninety-nine percent of the hours they were awake, we would think twice about road rage or the way we talk to people. Over the years, I've come to realize that there is a thin line between sane and insane and a grey area that we call normal.

So I needed to know what was it that kept me grounded when I really wanted to throw in the towel. What was so special about me that caused people to stand in awe as I walked through my daily journey? It is true that the daily load the average person contended with was equivalent to my morning start. The Army's slogan was my motto; because I really did more before day break then the average person did all day. I would wake up running and would not stop all day. After years of calling it my survival mode, I began to understand that it wasn't a mode; it was the Anointing of God. Yes, God's supernatural ability was there to do for me what I could not do for myself.

Reflecting over my life allowed me to see that I had actually gone further than I thought I could go, taken more stuff than I ever thought I could take, and had definitely done more than I could have ever imagined. That's why I'm still here, having gone through all that I've been through, still standing and praising God. Realizing that it wasn't anything super special about me or my choices, only God's power that showed up when I chose His plan for my life.

Throughout the Word of God there are many instances where men and women were able to do vast assignments when The Anointing was upon them. Samson was able to kill 1,000 men with the jawbone of an ass when the Spirit of God came upon him. David, even as a little lad defeated the giant Goliath, because of the Anointing. Moses was able to lead over a million people out of bondage and he could barely talk. Abraham and Sarah were old in their natural bodies but were able to conceive and birth the promise. These are just a few people that mixed God's super with their natural and were able to attain the supernatural. Unlike them we have the advantage, because no longer does the Anointing have to show up for a moment and leave, the Holy Spirit now lives inside of every believer. All we have to do is tap into it. It is the Anointing, nothing special about any of us; it covers all of our deficiencies. Let's take a think break and reflect on all of the things that we know that if it had not been for God, no way it would have happened. You know the real testimony; now let's take a shout break and thank God for His Anointing.

When my husband and I got married, many people prophelied (told false prophesies) that we would not make it through a year. I even had a very dear friend of mine to come to my house and tell me that he was not my husband. My mom tells him all the time, "I don't know how you put up with Shevelle." She knew her child, but failed to recognize that the only reason God had given me to her was because He knew that she could handle the task. Likewise, He presented me to my husband because He knew that he could handle the task. The reason why my husband and I have been married for eleven plus years is only because of the Anointing. I believe with all my heart that my Anointing is tailor made for that man. It blows my mind when people look to covet what God has joined together, having no clue about what really goes into the product that greets them daily. My mom always says that people see you but they have no idea. My interpretation is that there is a story behind the glory.

God has anointed each of us for the path that he has set before us. Be honest, some stuff you see other people deal with make you say, "It couldn't be me." But I've learned over the years that if it's in the plan, God will give you the power to endure, when others will be trying to jump ship.

I have a special tolerance to deal with my kids, as challenging as it may be, because of God's Anointing. I've learned how to depend on the Anointing to lead and guide me, to teach me what I don't know and to direct me when I'm unsure. Ever wonder why you haven't quit that job? Yep, it's the Anointing.

We have to become sensitive to the flow of The Anointing, because without notice the assignment can change and if you are not willing to make the transition, you'll be left to operate on your own.

My oldest sister, in my opinion is the epitome of a "Super Mom." I look at her in awe and wonder, "How does she do it?" She does it all, from getting the kids to school, herself to work, football practice, and all sorts of family drama in the midst, not to mention her health issues. She was able to do these things effortlessly until about three years ago. She had major surgery and endured some sort of complications that now causes her body to have seizures when she's gone beyond fatigue. God gave me a word to share with her in a meeting I was speaking at one night. He simply told me to tell her, "that which the devil meant for bad is working together for good; that He had established boundaries and she had to walk in her healing." I didn't understand the totality of what that meant, but I've learned to say what He tells me to say and do what He tells me to do. If He chooses to give me insight that's fine and dandy but if He chooses not to, He's still God. Later that week, God told me exactly what He was talking about concerning my sister. He revealed to me that the devil truly desired to kill her. The amount of stress that my sister functioned under was phenomenal. The sad reality is that many folks that operated under the same amount of stress she handled would have dropped dead with a massive heart attack. She just would not stop, so He had to run an interference, but we call it seizures. The whole process has truly taken its toll on her because of the type of person she is.

My sister is a cleaner and for the most part I'm not. I only clean because I have to. But Geessler is the type of person that always complains about having to clean up even when nothing is dirty. When we were growing up, I hated Saturday mornings, because after the cartoons would go off, it was spring cleaning every Saturday. I never wanted to dust, or mop, or sweep, and let's not talk about the bathroom. But not her, she would wake up with it on her mind and wouldn't stop until the job was completed. Well 30 plus years and 3 kids later, she maintained the tenacity to keep going, in spite of how tired she would be. We always joked about how different I am from both of my sisters; I know my limits and respect them. When I'm tired, I'm tired. Whatever is not done won't get done. Close the door. But not Geessler, she would rather have a tooth pulled before going to bed with a dirty dish. I'm not exaggerating; I would get tired just watching her work. I applaud her, because I knew it couldn't be me. She continued on for years, until her body couldn't take anymore. It screamed for rest and when the opportunity presented itself, it got it, and has vowed never to be pushed to the limit again. At this point in her life even when my sister wants to keep going, physically she shuts down.

I remember one weekend when my dad was living, my sisters and I decided to spend the weekend at my parents to do some spring cleaning. I left work, drove to Gretna to get Geessler, and got to my parent's about 10:30 that night. My thoughts were to get some grub and find a spot and call it a night, but not Geessler. That girl worked herself into a seizure, literally. I was convinced that the next day was going to be a light one, because of the drama the night before, but it turned out to be an instant replay. Later that week we chuckled about what happened. I told her that after watching her in action that weekend, I clearly understood why I hate cleaning; it was the fear of having a seizure. We had a good laugh.

My point is that no matter how anointed one is, know your limits and prepare yourself to hear from God for instructions and directions. God allowed the attack of the enemy because my sister ignored the warning signs. God had given her specific directions concerning her life, but she felt like she knew better than He what was best for her. Even though He allowed the attack, He still shielded her with His grace and mercy. Because of His divine plan for our lives, sometimes He has to protect us from ourselves. My sister still struggles with her new limitations but realizes now that God is in control.

The steps of a good man are ordered by God. So now when someone asks me the question, "How do you do what you do?" I boldly say, it's because of the Anointing of God. He has equipped me for the assignment. We have been anointed and appointed for such a time as this. Stay in your lane! Never petition God to be anointed like someone else. I've learned that Salvation is free, but the Anointing truly cost. The reality is that you have no idea what a person has gone through. Our prayer should be, "Lord, what is your will for my life?" Because it's only as we walk out His plan, that He will give us the power that we need. **THANK GOD FOR THE ANOINTING!**

CHAPTER THREE
ENJOY THE STATE THE LORD HAS CALLED YOU TO

...give thanks; for this is the will of God in Christ Jesus for you.
—1 Thess. 5:18 KJV

One thing that we have to be ever mindful of is that our roles are different. It is virtually impossible for me to think that as a married woman with two kids that I can function as a single woman with grown children. The reality is that if we're going to fulfill the plans and purposes that God has for our lives; we need to recognize what is required of us at this juncture.

I have a very dear friend named Jessica. She is single and her only son is in college. One day she called me to tell me that she had been angry with me for at least two weeks. Now it's one thing to be angry with a person and they are aware of it, but I think it's really ridiculous, when someone is angry with you and you don't even have a clue. This reminds me of another friend that I had. A day would not pass by that she and I did not talk at least ten times a day, and I'm not exaggerating. Something happened, and I noticed that she had not called me in a while. It seemed like the only time we conversed was when I called her, and those conversations would be extremely short because she was always busy. She would promise to call me back but that never happened. This went on for about two weeks, until one day I called her very humble I might add, to see if everything was okay. She got extremely testy and asked, "Why? Why shouldn't everything be okay?" Caught totally off guard, all I could say was "Okay, just checking." Now that should have been enough, but I called her again the next morning. Still humble and concerned, again I asked her if everything was okay and if I had done something to offend her. The response I got nearly floored me. She replied, "Well did you?" Once more I was at a loss for words and I told God that I was washing my hands of the situation because there was nothing else for me to do. About two months later I got a phone call from her and she was being her usual chipper self, asking about the kids, my husband, work, etc. After chatting for a few minutes she told me that she was calling to apologize because she had been angry with me for whatever reason. I listened very quietly, which for me was truly a challenge, because she was falsely accusing me. I wanted to tell her that she was lying, but the Holy Spirit would not allow me to say a word. But when He finally released me to speak, I remember asking God, is this you, are you sure you want me to handle this one, and I got the go ahead. Needless to say, she and I are now acquaintances. My point is that the Word of God clearly tells us how to handle a brother or sister that has offended us.

So when my girlfriend Jessica called me and told that she had been angry with me, I immediately had flashbacks but elected to handle things slightly different. She explained to me that it seemed like every time she asked me to go somewhere with her or to do something for her, I would always tell her, "I'll see and let you know." But every time I would ask her to do something she would be willing and waiting. She began to tell me about the time when her son graduated from high school and I didn't attend the party. Another time she wanted me to ride somewhere and I couldn't go, she went on and on. I had to be honest and admit to her that I understood how she felt, because for the first six or seven years of my marriage I had the same type of problem with my husband. Every time I would ask him to do something or go somewhere, rarely would he commit immediately. He would always tell me, I'll see and let you know, and that would bug me to no end. Because it seemed like every time he needed me to commit to something he was doing, I was always so willing. To add insult to injury, it always seemed like whenever someone else would ask him to do something, there would be no hesitation. I would be standing there wanting to scream, and would give him the *"how you gon,"* look. You know the **"how dare you"** look, or the **"wait until we get in the car"** look. Yea, **that look**.

I remember Thanksgiving, 2003; I had been asking my husband for weeks about our plans for the holiday. Because it always seemed like we could never get on the same page when it came time to decide where we were going to spend the holidays. As usual, I wanted us to go to my parent's that Wednesday night and spend Thanksgiving Day with them and come back home that Friday, but he would not give me a definite answer. Finally he told me that he just wanted to stay at home and probably do something with his little brother, because we had just placed his mom in a nursing facility and he wanted to hang around the house. He told me to take the kids and go, and if he felt up to it he would join us later. Me being the submissive and obedient wife that I am, took the kids and left, but even up to the moment that I left the office I was still asking him to join us. The kids and I made it to my parent's and I called Anthony about ten o'clock to see what he was doing. I could hear the wind in the background, so I asked him where was he headed, thinking he was just out for a ride. To my surprise he told me that he was on his way to his godmother's house to spend the night. Now I don't know if any of you have ever experienced a time when you get shocking news and it seems like the whole room disappears and all you see is the person's mouth moving, kind of like the cartoons do sometimes, well that's what happened to me. The room got black and all I could see were the words literally coming through the receiver of the phone. "How you gon," was probably the most censored part of the whole conversation. To me that was like a slap in the face, and it took months before my husband

Enjoy The State The Lord Has Called You To

and I could actually sit down and talk about what happened.

My ability to empathize with Jessica wasn't enough. Since she was my friend, I took a moment to explain to her how my household operates, and I stress mine, because every house is different. At 16978 Reiger Road, I am the primary and if need be secondary caregiver of my children. For years my mind was perplexed, because I could not for the life of me understand how my husband could get up, get himself ready, and go wherever he chose, without the stress of having to deal with our little people. He could go out to prayer in the morning and stay as long as he wanted. If he felt like he wanted to come home and take a nap, go to the gym, or head into the office, he had that liberty. Unfortunately for me, I didn't have that type of luxury, because when I headed out those doors for whatever reason, my kids were always with me. ***Me time*** was and is very limited. But after years of being frustrated, one day I ran across the Virtuous Woman in Proverbs. At first I thought it was a joke, no way could this be done, but then I began to allow the scripture to unfold. The fact of the matter is that God gave me to my husband to help him (my husband) meet his purpose. So whatever is needed of me to help him accomplish the goal, it's in me, I just have to pull it out.

When we initially got married, my husband and I made a pact that he would take care of the outside work and I would do the inside; which for the life of me, I can't figure out why I agreed to such a thing. I hated cleaning and pressing, and all of the other stuff that went along with housework, but before I knew it I found myself stuck in this treaty. Not to mention that my husband was no help, because he would pay people to cut the grass and wash the cars and do all the other stuff he was supposed to do. It got so bad until he reached a point where he wanted me to get me some help, but I was determined to show him that I could do it. I vowed to stick it out to the end but I couldn't do it. He got sick of looking at the clothes and the dishes and hunting for the remote. When my daddy was hospitalized in 2003, my husband had to take care of the kids and the house for a few weeks. When I returned home, I had someone coming in to clean for me two days a week and I must admit it felt good. My husband recognized that he needed a clean environment to be able to function better and my plate was full. It didn't make me any less of a woman to receive the help.

My point is that before I can obligate myself to anything, I have to make sure that those things that I am responsible for are covered. Trust me, I hear you and I feel your pain. Why? Why? Why? "You didn't make those kids by yourself, so why should you have to be the one to care for them with little or no support? Why do you have to check your schedule, he doesn't check with you?" The understanding that I received through the word of God and communicating with my husband is that I have to be able to fulfill that which he needs. There was a time in our marriage when we had to make a life changing decision that required us trusting God at a level that I didn't even know existed. My husband clearly explained to me what his greatest need was concerning his family. He didn't need a woman to bring home the bacon, but the rest of the story was on the money. The fry it up in the pan and the never, never let you forget you're a man, cause I'm a woman story. The reality is that he had no desire to be Mr. Mom. He gave me the option to stay at home while he followed after God and began his ministry. Not being able to conceive that notion, because we had just come out of a wilderness experience and mentally I was not up for another journey. Because he gave me the option, I opted to start a pharmacy, which allowed me the opportunity to have my kids at work with me, and for the most part that worked out great. We were able to support the things of God through revenues that were generated by the business, and still today that avenue is still open. To tell you that I enjoyed talking to little people all day long would be a lie, but I thank God for the opportunity to watch them grow. When my kids started pre-K, both of them were exceptional students and still are. My husband recognized that there were areas in his life that he lacked the skills and needed me to fulfill that void. He often alludes to the role my mother played in helping him choose me as his wife. My husband was able to see my mother's staying power and how she valued her family, and hoped that the apple did not fall far from the tree. When I got a clearer understanding of the totality of my role in my husband's life and his ability to fulfill the divine purpose that God has for our lives, it helped me to do, when I really didn't want to. Am I still frustrated from time to time? Yes! But I now understand that it is just dealing with the pressures of life and for the most part I get over it.

Taking the time to explain these things to my girlfriend Jessica enabled me to see that even though I might not have been there to go for a ride, or to hang out at her house, she knew that if she really needed me I had her back. Like the time when her son was in an automobile accident, she called me, and I was there. Even before she and I had established a friendship, just because she was a patient of mine, I remember leaving my pharmacy and not only delivering her medication but also making a Wal-mart run for her. But most important of all was when she was at the end of life's emotional road, God allowed me to be a vessel that was instrumental in helping her establish a relationship with Him.

We have to know, understand, and do our part. I often tell my single ladies to enjoy the state that God has called them to. Yes, the grass looks greener on the other side but everything that glitters is not gold. The extra maintenance helps to keep the shine.

Enjoy The State The Lord Has Called You To

A few years ago one of my girlfriends was getting married and we gave her a bridal shower. The whole crew was there and everyone had their advice, because all of us were married and felt like we had mastered the game. When it was my turn to give my words of wisdom, I simply told her that her life as she knew it was over. It was no longer about her; but her ability to aid her husband in birthing the purpose that God had placed in him. They thought I had lost my mind. Their replies ranged from, "It's about fifty-fifty," "You had a career before he found you." "You're, your own woman, and you have needs too!" I didn't argue my point; I spoke my peace and left it alone. Because what the rest of the crew didn't realize was that there is a huge difference in marrying a worldly man and a God fearing man. My friend's husband-to-be was a pastor and having walked and sometimes having to crawl that journey; I knew what was in store.

I got married at 28. I had been taking care of myself since high school. When my husband found me I had a furnished apartment, a car and a career. I was not needy in any shape, form, or fashion. Not to change the subject, but I need to really find out what does "shape, form, or fashion" mean. Growing up in the Baptist church I would hear that all the time. I never knew exactly what it meant, but when the older ladies would say it, it sounded like they meant business. With all of the accolades that went along with being a single, successful, black woman, there was still a need in my life. Not for companionship, because I had my fair share of all of that, but the desire to be able to share my heart, totally. The until death due we part stuff. The weird thing for me was that until I met my soul mate I never desired to be married, it all seemed like too much work. It wasn't until I met my husband that I realized how much I really desired to share my life with someone, the good, the bad, and the ugly. When we dated, I would always tell him that we were together by choice. I chose to be with him and he with me. It took a lot of getting used to, because I was and am very strong willed, but I now recognize the final authority in my home. Yes, I had to learn how to do the "S" word, no not sex, SUBMISSION. That taboo word that makes so many women decide to stay single their entire lives. Many of my ladies at the ministry ask me, "How do you do it?" I tell them that my submission is really unto God, my husband reaps the benefits. I submit to him as he submits to God, who is the one that is large and in charge. It blew my mind when my eyes were opened to the distinct difference between obeying and submitting. I really thought I was doing something when I obeyed my husband, despite the attitude that went along with it. One day I learned that submitting had nothing to do with doing or not, but the heart and mindset. I found out that it was possible to obey and not submit. At that point I had to start working on my heart and motives.

Enjoy The State The Lord Has Called You To

Sometimes it would get so bad until I would write down dates and times of decisions that my husband would make that I would not be in agreement with, only to have proof if and when things didn't work-out. Then one day I had to ask myself, what did I need proof for? If things didn't work out both of us would be affected, so instead of keeping score I began to pray for grace and mercy. After eleven years of marriage, I've learned to choose my battles. It hasn't always been easy but it has been worth it. Bottom line is that our lives are different, as well as our roles. Like it or not, it is what it is. Make the best of it.

    Enjoy the state that God has called you to for it is His will for your life. Maximize the moment because it could change at a moment's notice. My sister Tracey and I were talking one day and she began to share with me how she admired some decisions that I made and was even a little envious at the opportunities that I capitalized on. I got married and had children after I finished college. I really had an opportunity to enjoy me. When I was single I made the best of it. I enjoyed being able to go where I wanted to go. I shopped and traveled and didn't have to be responsible for anyone except me. As soon as that season was over, I was able to make the transition into being married. My husband always tells me that he wished we could have had an opportunity to enjoy being married a little longer before we had kids. I used to wish I had done it all a little sooner, but the reality is that if I had the opportunity to do anything different, I wouldn't. I was happy when I was single and now that I'm married with children, I'm even happier. When my babies are gone off to college I will be ecstatic. **KNOW YOUR ROLE AND PLAY IT.**

CHAPTER FOUR
DON'T LET PEOPLE PUT YOU IN A BOX

...ye shall know the truth, and the truth shall make you free.
—John 8:32 KJV

November 2003, taught me a valuable lesson that people want what they want and sometimes it may not always be in everyone's best interest. That year my father's birthday, which is the sixteenth, fell on a Sunday. Because of our service time on Sundays, riding to my parents after church was normally a push. Not only was my dad's birthday in November, but my mom's is on the tenth and my husband's the eleventh. November was always a busy month, so I always tried to devise a plan that permitted me to attempt to make all parties involved happy.

No one had etched out any plans for my parent's birthday, so I decided to drive down to visit with them the weekend before my mom's birthday because I had planned to do something special for my husband the following weekend.

Quite often I wonder if I am the only person on earth that has to deal with the, *he's just their dad syndrome*; referring to my husband, the father of my children. It took a while, but I had to explain to my family that the same love and admiration that I had for my daddy is the same that I desire for my kids to have towards their father. I don't know how or when it happened but at some point, it seemed as if our lives revolved around my family. Holidays, birthdays, just because days, the whole nine yards; almost as if he had no family. For years I thought it was a girly thing, but even as a kid I remember holidays when my brothers and their families would be at my parents the entire day, rotating holidays was unheard of. **Newsflash:** There has to be some compromise. If not dealt with, this thing could really cause a spirit of division that could wreck a home.

At any rate, I had my plan together. We took my mom to Café DuMonde's for beignets, hung out with her and my dad, and had a great time as usual. Spending time with my parents ranked in the top 3 things that I loved to do in my down time. Rarely did a week go by that I did not see them for at least a couple of hours, or two weeks that I did not spend at least one night to give my mom a break in caring for my dad. If I went longer than two weeks without seeing them I began to have withdrawal symptoms.

Most times my husband would be bored out of his mind when we would go to visit, but I enjoyed every moment. It was a place of rest for me. One day he and I had a discussion about why he didn't like to visit my parents. He explained to me that it wasn't that he had anything against them, truth be told, he loved them like they were his parents. Besides the drive time, his only problem was that I never wanted to do anything except sit around the house when we got there. I had to explain to him that when I decide to visit my parents, that's what I plan to do, visit (lie in their bed, eat on the sofa, listen to the same stories I've heard hundreds of times before, walk on the levy, sit on the porch) with my parents. He felt like I would ignore him and would give them 99.9% of my attention. I had to explain to him that it made no sense to me for us to drive two and a half hours to sit on my mom's sofa and talk to each other. My husband is an introvert around my family, even after 15 years, but I'm not, I enjoy the time that I spend with them very much. The reality is that for the most part I am available to my husband 24/7, now if he chooses not to capitalize on the moment, that's not my fault nor my parents.

Nevertheless, November 16th rolled around and my cell phone started ringing. Ironically, it wasn't from my mom or dad, but from several of my siblings, each asking the same question. "Are you coming to the country?" I had the same reply over and over, "No, not today." I went on to explain to each caller that I had already visited with my mom and dad and we had a terrific time. But it began to get a little taxing when I started hearing stuff like, "this might be my dad's last birthday," or "it always seems like you have something else to do instead of getting together with the family." I listened very intently and once more experienced the power of God and His ability to keep me, even when I didn't want to be kept.

I'm Not God, I'm Just a Woman

The reality is that my life was and is extremely hectic, but I realized years ago that no matter how demanding things are, making time to enjoy the simple things in life was a priority. I am forever grateful for the love, support and sacrifices that my parents have given to me my entire life. I've always felt like I had a unique mixture, because my parents were actually old enough to be my grandparents. Having only known my maternal grandmother, who died when I was at the threshold of life, and having the ability to find the wisdom that grandparents possess in my parents was truly a blessing. Taking the time to reassure them of my gratitude was high priority. I never wanted my parents to feel like they were a burden or that their labor was in vain. All they ever wanted was some of our time and that didn't cost much. The need for me to reassure my parents of how appreciative I was for having them in my life was something that I yearned to do, not just at Christmas or birthdays, or anniversaries, but year round.

At some point my husband and I had an eye-opener that has truly blessed our lives and finances. The first Christmas after we got married, we bought presents for everyone. We spent money that we truly didn't have; ran up charge cards and could barely pay our bills the next month. We could hardly wait to file our income taxes and probably would have done rapid refund, but we needed that extra $200.00. So we sat down and asked ourselves what was the logic in what we did. Having to make financial adjustments was probably one of the bigger adjustments for me when I got married, because I was accustomed to spending what I wanted, when I wanted and how I wanted. But my life was different; I had a husband and a newborn. The budget had changed and we had to make adjustments. So we agreed that we would not be driven by the world's standards of when we should show appreciation. We decided to position ourselves to hear from God and to be good stewards over that which He had blessed us with. Now I would love to tell you that that is how the story went, but I would be lying and there would be no truth in what I'm saying. But after we reached a point of being sick and tired of being sick and tired of paying on credit cards that balances would increase instead of decrease, we learned. The word of God teaches that, he who is faithful in little, He will make you ruler over much.

Long story short, I had already visited with my parents, but my siblings thought that wasn't good enough; they felt like I should have been there on the actual day of my dad's birthday, when they were available to visit. At one point in my life I would have given their concerns some thought, but at that junction their opinions were just that, their opinions.

I'm the youngest of ten kids and my family is very controlling and dominating. We all feel like it has to be our way or no way.

I'm Not God, I'm Just a Woman

When God began to transform me into a new creature in Him, it took a while for them to adjust. Just recently my sister Tracey shared some of the concerns that were hot on the wire about me. She said that Sunday after Sunday she had to defend my sanity, because they all thought I had lost my mind. Everyone felt like she knew that I had gone crazy but was covering up for me as usual. I think the most hilarious part of all was when she told me that she would have my back in front of them, but when she would get home, she would be so worried because even to her it seemed like I had wigged out a little bit.

Tracey and I were like Frick and Frack growing up. We were closer than two peas in a pod. If she said the sun rose in the west and set in the east, so be it. She was my mentor; often introducing me as the child that she didn't give birth to. I remember when the time came to draw the line in the sand concerning our relationship. It was my daughter Trinity's 1st birthday and we were having a birthday bash for her. Because of the number of people that we knew at the time, it was more feasible and economical to have her party at home in the yard. So excited about my first baby and the party, I called my siblings to invite them up to share in the momentous occasion. When I called Tracey, who's also Trinity's godmother, everything was everything until I told her to make sure that her husband did not bring any liquor with him, because we were not allowing it. This should have been a no-brainer right, kid's party, sodas, candy, cake; NOT! My family loves a party, they love to have a good time and they love to drink. When God delivered me from the spirit of alcohol, once more my family wasn't ready, but they eventually caught on.

When my husband and I got married we didn't want alcohol at our reception. Man you would have sworn that I had slapped my mom and dad and showed them my you know what. Those folks acted like donkeys. I had one of my brothers to tell me that if Anthony and I didn't want liquor at the reception, then we should have had a private wedding reception. Another said that the reception was not even for us (the bride and groom), but for the people, and the people out there wanted alcohol or they were not going to come; again, all sorts of craziness. Needless to say, they had cases and cases of liquor that they spent their money on, I wasn't happy, but my husband told me again to choose my battles.

Having to revisit this alcohol thing for Trinity's birthday party was not even open for discussion. So when I told sister girl (Tracey) about no alcohol, I expected 100% support in my favor, NOT! Girlfriend went *how-you-gon* so quick until my head started spinning on the phone. Long story short, only two of my siblings came to the party, but we still had a blast. My point is that no matter how much you love people, you can't afford to allow people to pressure you into doing something that you don't feel comfortable with or that goes against your beliefs.

The thing that the Holy Spirit showed me concerning my dad's birthday was that my siblings were not angry at me for not being there, but what angered them was the fact that I was not allowing them to manipulate or control me. When the real story came out, all of them had ulterior motives behind my trip to Phoenix that day. My sister didn't feel like fixing my dad's medication, because it could be a little time consuming. She was hoping that I was coming down and could take care of it. My brother's son needed a ride back to school and he was banking on him riding back with me. Which none of these things benefited me, but made their lives a little easier, and would not have been a problem if I had planned to go down there. Having spent many years watching the works of a controlling spirit from both ends of the spectrum, and finally getting to a point to take a stand against it, I refused to allow anyone to control me and I definitely was not trying to run anyone else's life.

My siblings and I often laugh about how our parents reared us. Even down to the way we refer to our parents, 'my momma' or 'my daddy'. What seemed so normal to us to other people seemed a little weird. When I was in college, one day my roommate asked me a question that almost got her bopped in the mouth. She overheard me talking to one of my sisters and we were laughing as usual and I asked her had she talked to my momma. I don't remember what my sister's reply was, but I do recall my roommate barely being able to wait until I got off the phone to ask me did we have different parents. Between the look I gave her and my response, she immediately clarified why she asked the question. She said that most normal people, when talking to a sibling about their parents do not refer to them as **my**, because they belong to everyone. I told her that apparently we were different and from our perspective, things were not going to change any time soon.

In all honesty my parents had so much love for all ten of their children that sometimes it seemed like you were an only child. By nature we are born leaders. My father was a leader and attributed most of his success to his soul mate and God's grace and mercy. We were far from being an average family. My father was very active in the political arena and was very instrumental in the civil right's movement in Plaquemines Parish. He headed up the Voter's Right Organization, which allowed black people to have the right to vote. Some of my older siblings were the first blacks to integrate the school system in our parish. Throughout life, we've all had to chase the ghost of other people's expectations and to be totally honest, it paid off. It paid off because you knew that you were expected to excel. Failure was not an option. To date, most of my siblings are in some form of management in their careers and are doing well.

I'm Not God, I'm Just a Woman

When my father died in 2004, we had an opportunity to see how crazy we all can be with little effort. It amazes me how death has a way of separating families, but in spite of all of our differences that whole experience brought us closer together. Being able to survive the All Chiefs no Indians episodes, of everyone wanting to be in charge of everything, was a task. It kind of reminded me of the automobile accident my father had in 1973, that left him disabled to some degree. Because my father was hospitalized for several months, my sister Tracey and I would have to stay home with some of our older brothers and each one felt like he was the man of the house. One would tell you yes and the other would say no. My mom was so exhausted from commuting to the hospital everyday, until she would allow the older siblings to make decisions concerning the youngest of the clan. When my father came out of the hospital and started recovering, there was no need for him to worry about disciplining us, because they had it covered. I remember my mom always saying, "Just wait until Dexter comes home." Dexter was my middle brother that was stationed in Mississippi and my mom would threaten us with him all the time. In my mind I would be thinking, what is Dexter supposed to do, that you can't do? He's not my daddy so he can't tell me what to do. (Remember I said I was thinking these things, not verbalizing them, okay maybe a little under my breath.)

Don't Let People Put You In a Box

Bottom line is that we were loved, never any question about how much. My husband often tells me that I am spoiled. I don't call it spoiled, I call it loved. My family was poor but we did not realize it, because there was never a lack of anything in my house. My parents and older brothers were very protective. We rarely had friends outside of each other, and to this day my siblings are still my closest friends. My two sisters would often tell me that if I wasn't their sister, they wouldn't be my friend. I know that they are just kidding, well maybe half kidding. I know they love me, because after all that I've put them through and still am putting them through, I know that they are just a phone call away.

Knowing how much my family loved me, and wanted what they thought was best for me, I still had to reach a point in my life when I had to make decisions for myself. Watching my sisters grow up and seeing the results of decisions they made to please other people, at their expense, was not about to happen to me. When my oldest sister Geessler went off to college she stayed with one of our aunts and every weekend she had to come home. She was not allowed to work, because my dad felt like that was going to disrupt her study time. My parents held on to her with tooth and nail, until it just got u-g-l-y. My sister Tracey also stayed with an aunt, but she was a little more sociable, but the home every weekend rule and no job, other than work study was still enforced. By the time I came along, I went against the grain. Both of my sisters went to Xavier University in New Orleans, but I went to Dillard University first and later transferred to Xavier. I told my parents that I wasn't staying with any relatives; instead, I was going to get a room on campus. I got a job and eventually got my own apartment. The biggest blow to my parents was when I joined the military. I remember calling my dad telling him what I had done and to inform him of my ship date for basic training; he told me that since I didn't have the decency to tell him about what I planned to do before I did it, there was no need to call him now. My mom felt strongly that the military was no place for a lady. She believed that only loose women joined the military and I'm not talking about the women that leave Bishop Jake's meetings. In spite of everyone's opinion, I knew what I needed to do for me. They eventually came around and were so proud of their little jewel.

For years I watched people chase 'The Ghost' of other folks expectations of how they should live their life and at the end of the road, most of them ended up being miserable.

It took me seven and a half years to complete a five year program in college. I had to make a decision to either worry about what people were going to say, have a mental breakdown, or reduce my hours to part-time to give my mind a break. I spun my wheels for a few years being distracted by the devices of the devil and his imps, but sooner than later, we (God and I) got it together. In the process of taking a quick inventory and developing a realistic plan to get where I wanted to be, it hit me one day. I was actually enjoying a lifestyle that most of my colleagues dreamed about. God had blessed me with my own luxury apartment, not some hole in the wall, typical college student apartment. I stayed in a gated apartment complex, where some of my professors lived. I had my own car and was able to work part-time and made more money than most people who worked full-time. Realizing that I wasn't on anyone's time schedule, except my own, I put my life on cruise control and continued to live.

One day, nearing the end of my last semester of summer school, my friend Sherie and I were in the admin building and we ran into one of my home girls. I was so excited to see her, but when she opened her mouth I could have put my foot it in. I could barely get hello out before she asked, "What are you still doing back here?" My girlfriend was so p'd. She was looking at me with that *how she gon* look on her face. I explained to my home girl that life is a process, some roads have a tendency to be a little lengthier than others, but they are all by choice. I assured her that life was great and that all my bills were paid. I felt a need to do that because apparently she was concerned about my well-being. Then I helped my girlfriend by explaining to her that she cannot allow other people's opinion of what she should do and how long it should take, be a factor in her life, especially when they are not paying her bills. The reality is that each of us have to be happy with the person in the mirror. That's the only person's destiny that we can control. People will always have their thoughts and concepts of how your life should be, but wisdom is always there to help you make the right decision.

Soon after I graduated from college, I went home to my parents to visit for a weekend, and as usual, we had a great time. When I was about to leave that Sunday evening to go back to New Orleans, I kissed my dad and he asked me where was I going. I explained to him that I was going home. He looked at me really puzzled and asked me what did I mean by home? I gently explained to him that my address was no longer at the red brick house that sits back on the lawn about half mile past Phoenix High School on Hwy 39; instead, my physical and mailing address was now 10501 Curran Blvd. in New Orleans. It took a little getting used to, but after seeing all that I had an opportunity to see, I wasn't quite ready to come back to the nest just yet, I wanted to continue to fly.

When I moved to Baton Rouge, my family really had mixed emotions. I had caused them to have to deal with so many other variables that they were not quite prepared for, until the thought of relocating to another city was not that big a deal, but it still didn't go over very well. At some point they recognized that I was going to do what I wanted to anyway, so for the most part they were supportive in a weird way. I had to reach a point where I had to make decisions that were in my best interest. Some people may have felt like I was being selfish, but I realized that if I didn't look out for my best interest and take charge of my destiny, who would.

It is imperative that we set ourselves to hear from God. As He gives directives we have to carry them out. People will always have their thoughts and concepts; line them up with the word of God. Take charge of your life and watch God move. We have to always be watchful, because the enemy will try any tactic and use anyone he can to keep God's people in bondage. It's time to stop allowing people to put you in a box with their thoughts and opinions, **GET OUT OF THE BOX!**

I'm Not God, I'm Just a Woman

CHAPTER FIVE
JUST BECAUSE YOU'RE INVITED, DOES'NT MEAN YOU HAVE TO GO

To every thing there is a season…
a time to embrace, and a time to refrain from embracing.
—Ecclesiastes 3:1, 5

    I am the youngest of ten children, my mother is an only child, but my father had eleven siblings. We have over 50 nieces and nephews, not including greats; over 70 first cousins and eons of second, third, and fourth. My husband has six siblings and oodles of aunts, uncles, and cousins that I've never met. We have an extended church family, a business, and two little people that we live with, who allow us to be their parents. With all of this in mind, it is virtually impossible for me to attend every birthday party, wedding, funeral, graduation, prom, holiday dinner, baby shower, etc. It just won't happen. For years I made a conscious effort, putting my best foot forward, until the doctor explained to me that the pains in my chest were primarily caused by anxiety and stress. He informed me that my body was tired and if I didn't slow down, it was going to quit on me. Leaving his office feeling pretty overwhelmed, because so much responsibility hinged on me, and convinced that if I didn't do it, chances were great that stuff was not going to get done; as a result, the stressing process began all over again.

    The need to make some adjustments in my day to day activities left little room for a social life. Coming to grips with the reality that I was no longer able to be one of those people that graced every event with my presence, even if I did get there late, was a process. Not to be facetious, but I actually know people like that. No matter what it is or where it's at, you can always count on them to be there, and on time. For the life of me, I don't know how they do it. In spite of all my efforts, I still managed to get to everything late. Despondent because the wedding would be over, the casket closed at the funeral, benediction gone forth at the graduation, and so on. Aside from everything else, I think the absolute worse part of all would be the late again look that people would give me, as if I purposely planned to make my grand entrance, late.

Before I had kids, things were not as bad, but after they came along, anything that involved mobility via an automobile was a chore. Remembering how guilty I would feel if someone invited me to something and I didn't go, especially when I gave my word to be there. It never failed, I would make all sorts of plans to attend, but just as sure as my name is what it is, something always came up. And the few times that we were able to go, having to hear about all the other times that we didn't show up, didn't help. It would be pandemonium if I went to one of my nieces' birthday party and did not make it to another, or if one member of my staff had an event that I was able to attend, but a few weeks later could not attend

Just Because You're Invited, Does'nt Mean You Have To Go

another's. It would cause so much chaos, until I reached a point that I said the heck with it, and just stayed at home.

Not having to push myself into what I call my **press-mode** felt good for a season, until I realized that the invites had stopped. My sister Tracey had a birthday party and when I found out about the party, it was over. Bear in mind, that this is the same heifer that I talk to everyday. She figured I wasn't going to come anyway, so why bother. The nerve of her, I felt like she should have at least given me the opportunity to make my own decision. My feelings were hurt and I really felt bad. It wasn't that I was trying to win the **Ms. Anti-Social of the Year** award; I just didn't know what else to do.

My siblings and friends felt like I had abandoned them for "those people in Jackson" (my church family). My church family felt like I really didn't love them because I wouldn't attend anything that wasn't required of me. It was all a hot mess. One day I was in Wal-mart and I saw one of my girlfriends/ex-coworkers from Walgreens. She and the rest of the crew, felt like I had thrown them away. I tried to explain to her how busy things were and that I had made several attempts to reach out to her but all I ever got was an answering machine. I did leave messages but never got a return call. She went on and on and I listened and apologized but nothing seemed to help. After leaving my friend that day I started reflecting over my life, attempting to figure out what changed, when and how. Things were different, my focus was not the same; years had actually passed by and it seemed like days. What happened? I know, Purpose was birth!

When I left Walgreens, after my husband was called away from his government job into full time ministry, our family still had to eat. Everyone thought we had lost our minds and wondered how we were going to make it. My husband and I had a plan and it was up to us to make it happen. We had to do some major lifestyle adjustments. For a very long time we had no set schedule, no help, and no money, nothing but each other. The launch of our business was not easy. It was not just a business it was my personal ministry. Recalling times when I would be in my bed asleep and if a customer called, I went. Filling prescriptions from nine to five, or whatever time I would get there, and at five o'clock the delivery crew (Anthony, Trinity, A.J., and myself) would start rolling. Some days we would not get back home until midnight, and would get up the next day and do it all over again. Our family motto was, *"As long as we are together that's all that matters."*

The season had changed and we were operating in a zone that was unfamiliar to both of us. Many times we couldn't explain to people what was going on because we didn't know ourselves. We went to one of Bishop T.D. Jakes pastor and leadership

Just Because You're Invited, Does'nt Mean You Have To Go

conferences and he ministered on *Redefining Normal*. That place where things were comfortable (paid holidays, a savings account, sick days, vacations, health insurance, a routine). I can still remember the mornings that I would wake up, literally wondering where am I, because nothing about my life looked familiar. At one point it all seemed so bazaar, because we were so far out there, no chance of turning back, all eyes on you, sink or swim. So we started swimming, left stroke, right, back, whatever we had to do to make it happen, and it cost a lot of time and energy. Many times after I finished doing all that I could and thanking God for His grace to complete what was left over the next day, I didn't want to go anywhere except to bed.

In 2000, I bought a brand new Eddie Bauer Expedition. In one year I had driven over 50,000 miles, which some may not think is a lot, but I also had two other vehicles that I was driving as well, now that was a problem. Realizing that all of the ripping and running was not just taking its toll on my vehicles, but that it was literally wearing me down, forced me to do things a little different. Getting a new car was an option in a few years, even finding new friends, but I was the only one of me that I had. In the process of trying to find some sort of medium that would avoid me being ex-communicated from my family and friends, it hit me all at once like a ton of bricks. Just because you're invited doesn't mean you have to go, and if it means not getting the invites anymore, so be it.

Receiving that word of wisdom caused the weights to be lifted immediately. I felt liberated. Ironically, I became more and more like my husband, when it came down to committing to anything. It is true, that after you have been married to someone for so long you become like them. I practically lived in the play-it-by-ear zone, which helped me out greatly. If something was going on and I felt up to it, I went, and if I didn't feel like going for whatever reason, I stayed at home.

There has to be a level of maturity amongst family and friends. It makes no sense to hold people in your heart over something as silly as a party. Yes, people get angry and end friendships over birthday parties. No, the party is not silly, but to get mad at someone because they didn't show up and then to commit in your heart that the next time they have something, you're not going, is CRAZY. You don't know what's going on in a person's life at a particular time. There have been times when my husband and I have been dressed, ready to walk out the door and the enemy shows its ugly head and before long I'm at home, my husband's gone, and the enemy is laughing. Sometimes the Holy Spirit will tell you don't go. At that moment you have to make a decision, to either take heed to the Spirit and risk sounding crazy to others, or worry about people's opinions and end up in a pickle. My husband's great grandmother died a few years ago and because of some friction amongst the family, I was a little concerned about how it was all going to play out. The morning of the funeral, my husband told me that he wasn't going. For a moment I thought, this guy is really out there. But later he explained to me that the Holy Spirit had warned him not to go. He didn't go, and it turned out for the best.

There is a selfish streak in all of us that drives us to want what we want. Several months ago my sister-in-law called me in a frenzy because we didn't attend her graduation in Chicago. In addition to having a prior engagement in Los Angeles, I wasn't even aware that she was graduating. Contrary to disbeliefs, I'm not that much of a brute; I would have at least sent a card, a text, or something. She informed me that my husband knew and assumed that he had given me the information. Why do people do that? Give messages to people that don't relay messages. I get so tired of hearing, he didn't tell you! After about the fifth time it becomes a little redundant. Anyway, girlfriend was steaming, because we were not there to celebrate her accomplishment. After chatting with her for a moment, I shared a little secret with her that has helped me on this journey that we call life. Explaining to her that sometimes people are not going to be able to do what you want them to do, when and how you expect them to. In other words, people are apt to let you down from time to time for whatever reason. In spite of who is, or is not there, you have to make the best of the moment. Sharing with her what I thought was the loneliest moment in my entire adult life, and I stress "thought," because since that time life has dealt me some pretty lonely moments. This particular incident was when I gave birth to my son, A.J. What should have been a very joyous occasion for whatever reason seemed to be very gloomy. When I had Trinity my whole family was there. I went into labor about eleven o'clock that Friday night and we got to New Orleans about one o'clock in the morning. By day break I had a lobby full of people, phone ringing off the hook, the whole nine yards. Trinity was born about 4:00 p.m. that Saturday evening and everyone was there to offer their advice and support. When I got pregnant with A.J., I decided to deliver him in Baton Rouge for whatever reason, probably just plain old logic. Well that worked out great for me and my husband, but my family was not available to come up on the day I delivered, because it was on a Wednesday. Only one of my brothers was there and my husband's godmother. In the hospital where I gave birth, they had a room that they rolled the mom and the new baby into, so that the family could see the new baby and meet the doctor. After my delivery, they rolled me into this room, but no one was there. I felt so abandoned; I could have and probably did cry. Realizing that very instant that it was my moment with my new baby, so what if no one else was there to rejoice. I was there, he

Just Because You're Invited, Does'nt Mean You Have To Go

was healthy, and that really was enough. When I began to re-direct my energy and focus to the correct channel, everything began to flow much better.

After sharing all of that with my sister-in-law, who I might add was not at the hospital for neither of my kid's births, nor my wedding to her brother, she understood my point, but she chose to still have a tude. The reality is that some changes come with time; I'm a witness. God has done and is doing a great work in me. My biggest struggle is recognizing and accepting that it's not always about me and what I want. The same level of maturity that I expect from others has to be reciprocated. Accountability is the key. If I'm not able to do something, I at least owe the next person the courtesy to inform them. It is totally up to them to receive it. **REAL FRIENDSHIP DOES NOT KEEP SCORE.**

I'm Not God, I'm Just a Woman

CHAPTER SIX
I'M TOO TIRED

Come unto me, all ye that labor and are heavy laden, and I will give you rest.
—*Matthew 11:28 KJV*

The most critical place a woman can find herself in is a state of tiredness; especially when it concerns those things that have been placed in her care. In lieu of the hustle and bustle of life, we cannot afford to run ourselves ragged. Juggling all that we juggle, it is imperative that we don't drop something that is essential. As a married woman I cannot afford to get so caught up in work, the kids, ministry, other folk's drama, family and friends that I forget about my duties as a wife. There are some things that I don't need anyone to help me with. You can pick up my kids and even wash some clothes for me, I might even eat some grub that you've prepared, but when it comes to my man, I don't need your help sister love, but I do need some rest.

When I had my first baby, in addition to the transition that my body had gone through, I nearly ended up in divorce court for irreconcilable differences; I was too tired to make love to my husband. Really I was. I nursed my baby and when she wasn't nursing it always seemed like he wanted to nurse. Convinced that something had gone wrong during my delivery, because before I had the baby, sex was great, but afterwards, it became a chore, led me to seek medical advice. My doctor explained to me that in addition to the hormonal changes that had taken place, I just needed to get some rest, "slow it down and take it easy, everything will bounce back," he added. Finding a balance worked out great, so much so until 20 months later I had another baby. By that time I really felt like I had lost my mind. Having two babies barely 20 months apart, and little to no help from my loving husband nearly tipped me over, because it never ended. There was always something or someone that needed my attention. I admire all mothers across the land, but to the stair-step moms, I have to give you your props; I don't know how you do it. I remember sitting in my bathtub, shortly after I had my son, weeping, because it was all a bit much. Having a limited support team left the bulk of the task up to me. As long as I was moving I was okay, but as soon as I stopped, where I laid was where I stayed. My husband would get so angry with me and would allow the enemy to convince him that for me to fall asleep was a form of rejection. **REJECTION! HELL I WAS TIRED!** I'm sorry, I'm okay, I just had a flashback. Tired was an understatement, I was worn out.

For the most part, I've always been a person that after a certain time of night my body shuts down. Even in college, I can remember the night before tests, people would pull all niters' to prepare, not me. What I didn't get by 10 o'clock, would not be

I'm Too Tired

gotten. Anyone that knows anything about me will vouch that I am not a night owl. I will fall asleep talking to you, honestly. But my husband is the total opposite. He could stay up all day and night if need be, and would get mad at me for going to sleep at a decent time. God forbid if I gave him any inkling that I might be up to a booty call and went to sleep instead; I lived in fear of the burning bed constantly.

Now, the truth of the matter is that I would attempt to do too much and the one thing that was required, I just could not seem to muster up the energy to do what was needed. We would have knock down drag-out fights concerning our love life. I was and am definitely a morning person, but he was more or less a night owl. When I went to sleep, please do not wake me for anything. Sleep was vitally important to me, and for whatever reason I viewed sex as work. This went on for months and possibly years, because in my mind I was able to justify that my husband was so selfish and that he had little regards for my needs. And then one day it happened. The light bulb was turned on and I was able to see the enemy and the liberty that I was giving him in my marriage. Maybe mine is an isolated case, but I get so tired of being able to identify, I'm talking putting my finger right on him (devil), but yet feeling helpless. It made absolutely no sense for me to think that it was okay for me to continue to neglect my husband's needs. Yes, it was neglect, because if I was able to find the time and energy to cook, clean, shop, visit, sleep and eat, then I could find the time and energy to be intimate with my husband.

One night some of the ladies in our ministry and I were at the church and everyone had the same complaint about not having the energy to do their wifely duties. We began to reminisce about the days of old when all niters would happen and how we would wear the teddies, feel the anticipation and was excited. Before I knew it I said it seems like we got married and then got saved. Everyone was looking at me a little strange, trying to figure out what that meant. I explained to them that before we married our mates we had no boundaries. (Ooops! Please forgive me, God has.) We were freaks! But after we got married, we (Saved women of God) felt like we were now too holy, too tired, and too busy, and that sex was something that we could do without. As opposed to dealing with the fact that it's the enemy, coming after our marriages to destroy them anyway he can, and sad to say, we are giving him all the ammunition that he needs. News flash: If you find yourself taking an extra long bath in hopes that he's asleep when you're done, that's not good. If you're in the living room half asleep waiting for him to start snoring so you can ease in the bed, watch yourself. If you purposely wear stuff to bed that you know will turn him off, you're on the wrong team. Can someone say ammunition?

I'm Too Tired

I remember telling my husband a joke that I heard, because it cracked me up so much I just couldn't keep it to myself. The joke was about a man who wanted to make love to his wife but she told him that she just wanted him to hold her instead and he did. This went on for a couple of nights and the husband decided that he wasn't going to get upset as usual, instead he was going to take her shopping. He got up one morning and told his wife that he wanted to do something very special for her and they went to the mall. By this time the wife's mind was blown that he would even suggest going anywhere with her, because normally if she didn't take care of his needs, he would be so p'd, but she was excited that both of them had grown and that he was learning to understand her needs and respect them. They got to the mall and went to her favorite store and she was looking at him trying to figure out what her limit was. Before she could ask the question he told her, "get whatever you want, don't worry about the cost." She became like a kid in a candy store and had stuff everywhere. She got to the counter and the cashier rang up the clothes and told her the total. The lady then turned to her husband for the money and he told her, "No, I didn't want you to actually get anything; I just wanted you to hold them." Of course my husband thought the whole thing was so funny.

We cannot get so distracted by life that we forget about our spouse. We are the outlet that they choose, trust me, there are several options available, but you are his choice. Make the adjustments. My husband hates me doing anything that will affect my ability to take care of his needs or cuts into his intimate time.

    I love to cook, hate to clean, but love to cook. Cooking to me is an art that I feel like I've mastered. It relaxes me. Seeing the look on people's faces when their taste buds are flabbergasted is priceless. The problem is that I can't do anything simple. Breakfast, lunch, dinner, snack, it all goes to another level. My sister-in-law always teases me about how long it takes me to prepare a meal. What's funny to me is that no matter how long it takes, they sit there waiting patiently. My husband and I would always entertain. Most of our friends would just want to come over so that I could cook. Very seldom would we be invited to go to their houses. Eventually my husband put a stop to it, because what would happen is that I would spend all day or night cooking, did little entertaining, and would be too tired to do anything else. Sundays were the same way. After church I would prepare Sunday dinner old school style. He shut that down too. Wisdom finally kicked in and I began to see my husband's point of view. It wasn't that he was trying to control me in some weird way, but he had needs that he needed his wife to meet. He chose not to find it in another woman and I am so thankful to God for keeping him. Even when I was at a point when I told him to go find him a Delilah, or a Jezebel, or even a Hagar, just to

I'm Too Tired

leave me alone. I've never had **wisdom** to step into the room the way it did that day. The Holy Spirit was slapping me in the face, as if to say, "enough is enough." I retracted that statement so quick my head was spinning. It was at that point I decided to take a look at what was really going on. My husband loved me and wanted me, not another woman. When I really thought about it, I did not have a problem, unlike some people I knew. One of my friends had to take anti-depressants, because every time her husband wanted to be intimate, she got depressed and they both started crying. Another friend felt like her love life lacked intimacy; her husband always did the *wham-bam-thank ya ma'am*. Another friend married an older guy and Viagra was her best friend. Recognizing that I had a young man that loved the Lord and his wife, I made adjustments and life is great.

    Even with our kids, having a headache or feeling the need to take a nap everyday all day is unacceptable. Our little people need us to play an active role in their lives, especially our minor children, and I stress minor. *Proverbs 22: 6* reads: *train up a child in the way he should go: and when he is old, he will not depart from it.* If you are still training a twenty-five year old baby something is wrong. It breaks my heart to see women that get stuck in the cycle of rearing children, grand-children and even great grand-children. At some point we have to regain control of our lives. My husband

and I started telling our kids that at eighteen they have to go. To college, the military, work, abroad, somewhere, anywhere, they just have to get out of our house. Some of our friends thought we were ruthless, but the motive is to get them to start thinking about a plan for their future. It was so embedded in them, until every time someone ask them their age, immediately they would do the math and add, "and I have x,y,z number of years left at home." Now, are we really going to give them a portion of their heritage and kick them out, probably not, but they don't need to know that.

Our lives are extremely demanding and require a sacrifice from the entire family, so we have to put forth a conscious effort to capitalize on the time we have with our little people. Children are a gift from God. We have them for a number of years to impart a measure of wisdom and knowledge that will last them a lifetime. I cannot get so wrapped up in the process, that I lose focus on the main reason why I do what I do. They need our time and attention. One thing that I've observed in my involvement with children is that they do not act out because they have nothing else to do. In most situations they are crying out for attention. When I get too busy with work or ministry my kids have a way of getting my attention and it's not always pretty.

I have a friend who's a single parent and her only son gives her the blues. She would always tell me that she does not understand what the problem is. She buys him stuff, works hard to give him a good life, and lives a christian life before him, but she still cannot reach him. One day I asked her when was the last time she and he had done some real one-on-one time; maybe to the park, the movie, or to the store, alone. She thought for a moment and realized that rarely are they alone when they do anything. For whatever reason, someone else is always tagging along. I told her to try something simple and see what happens. Sharing with her the grief my kids would give me if I took them to the store and talked on the cell phone the entire time we were together. Or if I planned to go somewhere with them and invited someone along and expected them to entertain themselves. Everyone would come home with a headache. After years of the drama, I had to make some adjustments for my own sanity. When the kids and I are together, I minimize talking on the cell phone, especially when I pick them up from school. Think about it, they have not seen me all day, and want to update me on what happened in the past eight hours. I found little questions to start a dialogue, recognizing that if I give them my attention without them pulling for it, I'm able to control the flow a little better. "How was your day," or "Did anything happen that I need to be aware of?" normally starts a conversation that lasts about 30 minutes. I've learned that I can either give those 30 minutes up front or have the rest of the evening full of them frustrating me and me them. When I plan to do something with my kids, and if I invite someone to tag along, they have to be kid friendly. One of my girlfriends will tell you up front that she does not like kids. If I'm planning a day with my little people, chances are great that she is not going to be invited.

When Trinity was a toddler, one of my friends came down to visit with us and the heifer almost got put out because of my daughter. She had a problem with my baby wanting my attention and even had the audacity to question why my husband couldn't tend to her. Needless to say, I moved, changed my number and did not send her any updated information.

Bottom line is that we cannot afford to make our little jewels feel like they are a bother. They need us. They watch everything we do and mimic what they will. If we do not sow good seeds into their lives now, how can we expect a good harvest? I refuse to reap anything different than what I've sown into my children's lives. As I continue to sow my time and God's wisdom, I'm not expecting at sixteen for him or her to shut down and decide that they want to rebel against life; the devil is a lie, and the father thereof. Next to wanting to operate in God's will for my life, my family is the number one reason that I get up each day and do what I do. But it makes no sense if after doing all that I think is needed I'm not giving them what they really want, ME.

Because our schedule can get really hectic, we schedule at least one day a week that we call family night and we bond as a family. Saturdays belongs to the kids. Recently my daughter decided that she wanted to take dance lessons and both she and my son wanted to play little league basketball. Monday, Tuesday, and Thursday evenings, plus Saturday mornings were dedicated to dance and basketball, and did I add that my husband and I coached the little league team. Yes, it was a stretch, but everything we do is a sacrifice. The reality is that we make the sacrifice wherever we want to, for me I choose to put what I can inside those little people that I live with while I have a chance. I cannot afford to cut corners any longer at my family's expense. I have an obligation that supersedes my role as a pharmacist, first lady, sister, evangelist, or daughter. I have to be mom, best friend, mentor, and disciplinarian to Trinity. A.J. calls me his favorite girl and when he wants to be mannish he calls me Sheryl, but will call me momma at the drop of a hat if something is wrong.

Stewardship, it goes beyond our families. Whatever God has placed in our care, has been given to us with an expectancy that we will be productive. I understand now that I cannot be effective in the things of God if I do not get my proper rest. A few months ago, my husband incorporated a "sundown" policy for the church staff. Basically, we attempt to shut down shop by sundown on Saturday in preparation for Sunday Worship service. Reason being, many of us would drag in late on Sunday mornings, in a funk and instead of us ministering to others, people would have to pump us up.

Rest is vitally important to a successful day. It's when I have not gotten my proper rest that I'm a beast to be around. The least little thing sets me off. For a long time I would ignore the signs and get into the press mode, but after a few episodes that were not pretty, I've learned. Nowadays, when I remotely feel like I'm creeping into the Red Zone, I tell myself to go to bed. Whatever it is that God has placed in your hands, he holds you accountable. **STOP THE MADNESS AND GET SOME REST.**

CHAPTER SEVEN
Finally

Finally…whatsoever things are true, whatsoever things are just, whatsoever things are pure…think on these things.
—Phil 4:8 KJV

I would love to tell you that I've discovered the one, two, three method to help you get it together and keep it together, but I haven't. The reality is that our lives are different and what works for me might not work for you. Though the demand is different there are some common factors that are beneficial to all. One thing for sure is that each of us have to identify what is expected regarding the many roles that we play. Whether married or single, children or not, there are many things that have to be taken into account.

Let's start with my single sisters, because heaven knows my life was far less complicated before I gained the responsibility of a family. If you are single and do not have any minor children, I have a request of you, that will ultimately bless your life. I need you to prepare yourself an elegant dinner, fine wine, china, candles, flowers, the works, and when you finish eating, break the plate. Breaking the plate is symbolic of how free you are. I'm aware that singleness has its positives and negatives, but the bottom line is that you're in control of you. In addition to taking this time to work on your personal issues, your primary focus should be building the Kingdom of God. Paul writes in *1 Cor. 7:7, For I would that all men were even as I myself...* Paul was single, and his singleness afforded him the opportunity to preach the Gospel, and build the people of God without any reservations. Please do not miss your opportunity to be a blessing to the body of Christ, while playing house with someone that is only reaping the benefits without accepting the responsibility.

For those of us that are married, not to mention married with children, our primary responsibility is to aide our husbands in fulfilling their God given purpose. Everything else that we do has to hinge on this concept. Whatever he asks of you, as long as it's not immoral, illegal or illicit, just do it. Charity clearly begins at home. My personal thought is that if I can't serve him, ain't nobody getting served. He is the authority in my life and before I do anything for anyone else, I have to make sure that he's covered. Adding kids to the equation is a little tricky and requires lots of communication. When my kids were babies they were my number one priority, wrong or right, the verdict is still out. They had no way of caring for themselves. I was at their beck and call to clothe, feed, change, and protect them. There was no such thing as ignore them, if they needed me I was there. Too often I felt the tug-of-war for my attention between my kids and my husband and most times he lost. Honestly, I felt like my husband had unrealistic expectations. But now that they are a little older, they understand mommy and daddy time. It took a lot of getting used to, but nowadays I can shut my door, or

Finally

send them to their room, and tell them do not disturb me unless it's an emergency. It's funny to see them still attempt to compete for my attention, but I have no problem letting them know who the boss is.

Maintaining a **balance** between the kids and my husband is crucial. I try to avoid either party having to pull for my attention. I never had the luxury of a strong support team after I moved to Baton Rouge, so I had to make the best with what I had. My outlets are minimal, which forces me to capitalize on any opportunity I can get, to take a break. For the most part my kids have to be in bed by nine o'clock. After a certain time of night I cannot bear to hear the pitter-patter of little feet. This is not only beneficial to them, to ensure that they get their proper rest, but it gives me a chance to unwind from my day, as well as spend some quiet time with my hubby. This is a house rule, and the few rules we have cannot be broken. If my kids have company over, they know that after a certain time, they have to shut it down. You'll be surprised the difference a few hours of quiet time will make.

We have already established the importance of rest, but allow me to add the other **R** word, relaxation. When the opportunity presents itself and my kids are away, I'm very selective about what I want to do and who I want to do it with. I go into what I call my **NO KIDS ALLOWED ZONE**. In other words, I'm not trying to be entertained with someone else's children, it's not happening. Because my husband and I relax totally different, sometimes this would cause a problem. For the longest; almost every time we got rid of the kids for any length of time, the enemy would show its ugly head. My plans would include dinner or possibly a movie, but lounging was at the top on my list. My husband on the other hand would want to go four-wheeler riding, car shopping, bowling or something, anything to get out of the house. He is an outdoor person and even though I like outdoors, my choice is a controlled climate. Over the years we have learned how to respect the other person's space, likes and dislikes.

There is always going to be some sort of pull, be it our children, spouse, ministry, friends, or family, somebody is always going to have a need. I've reached a point in my life that I can tell people to stop pulling on me for a moment. My husband and I have a staff of wonderful people that are like our children. A few months ago we had a wave of trouble that attacked the ministry from every angle possible, and it seemed like I had to wear so many hats and be several things to many people. Not fasting and praying like I needed to be left me open spiritually, and some of those spirits began to attach themselves to me. My husband, being the prophet that he is, was able to recognize what was going on and nipped it in the bud. Immediately, I became offended and thought that he was being

Finally

controlling, which was a side of him I had never seen before. But he was only trying to protect himself and me. Sooner than later I understood exactly what he was talking about. My primary ministry is to my husband, not to the church. I offer my ear as much as possible, but when it's time to back up, I know my place.

Planning is an area of my life that is under construction. According to the blueprints, organization is in the plan. Every morning I get up between 4:30 and 5 o'clock. After devotion and prayer, I get to the gym about 5:30, and normally I'm back home by 6:45a.m. Can someone help me find that **one** minute that I lose every morning? My kids have to be at school for 8:30a.m., but it never fails, 8:31 we're at drop-off.

My husband and I have to drive separate cars to church, because I'm never on time. I don't know about anyone else but I'm tired of running. The few times that I've managed to be on time, really felt good. Let's not even talk about early, oh my goodness. I know exactly what my problem is and I'm making a conscious effort to do better. Sunday mornings is not the time to try to start washing clothes and cleaning up. **Press the night before**. I have a girlfriend that lays out everything the night before, even down to the belts in pants loops for her kids. She's a single mom, but runs circles around me. A few months ago she had surgery and it blew my mind when she ordered and paid for pizza on Monday to be delivered on

Thursday. My poor babies would have been on their own, ramen noodles cuisine, ready in five minutes or less.

Technology is great. Recently I started using Outlook on my computer, because I'm noticing that as I get older, I'm not even trying to clutter my mind with a whole lot of stuff. Lately, I had to make some changes in the way I conduct business to aide me in transitioning into my different roles. My patients at the pharmacy are spoiled. All of them have my cell phone number and they have no problem using it. As a result, I would get the craziest calls at the most inopportune times. Limiting calls to emergencies only has made life easier. Leaving work at work helps me to focus on the needs of my family when I'm at home.

Delegate as much as possible. My son knows that he is responsible for taking out the trash. Although Trinity is lazy, if I could just get her to keep her room straight, I'll be satisfied. The more responsibility I give them, the freer my hands are.

Know your resources. At my office I used to attempt to do everything, because for so long I had to do everything. Then one day I asked myself why not allocate some of the responsibilities. If I'm going to do it all, why do I need employees? Electing to macro verses micro-managing has enabled me to be much more effective. Even in ministry, for years I thought I had to do it all. After eight years I've learned to welcome the help. I'm maturing to

Finally

a point that I am able to recognize the source of my stress and can now make a conscious effort to get rid of it. It's taken some time and energy, but the reward has been priceless.

Finally, **we have to become Kingdom minded.** *Matthew 6:33, says, "But seek ye first the kingdom of God, and his righteousness; and all these things shall be added unto you."* It took years for me to get the gist of what the writer was talking about. I had heard it preached forever and a day, to seek ye first the Kingdom of God, but no one ever told me exactly what it was. Maybe they didn't know. So I began to dig into the text and I got my own interpretation. Not many verses preceding verse 33 in the same chapter of Matthew, the writer writes about clothing and food and not worrying. So I thought I could find the Kingdom of God in the mall, and I shopped until I dropped thinking that it was in a particular style, NOT. Convinced that I could fill that void in my life with food, I ate at some of the finest restaurants, but that didn't help. I went into a carefree mode, and that was a mess. Then one night, my husband (then boyfriend) and I went to a meeting and the man of God ministered on the Kingdom of God. *Romans 14:17NKJV reads ... the Kingdom of God is not eating and drinking, but righteousness, peace, and joy in the Holy Ghost.* As women, we have to seek first the righteousness, peace, and joy of the Lord. When our priority becomes spiritual, God will meet every need in our lives. That's right, you're not God, **YOU ARE JUST A WOMAN!**

Use this convenient form to order additional copies of

I'm Not God, I'm Just A Woman!

Please Print:

Name_____

Address_____

City_____ State_____

Zip_____ Phone (   ) _____

E-mail_____

_____copies of book @ $12.95 each $_____

Postage and handling @ $_____ per book $_____

LA residents add 9% tax $_____

Total amount enclosed $_____

Make checks payable to:
Red Sea Productions

Send to:
**Red Sea Productions
P.O. Box 86028, Baton Rouge, LA 70879**

(225) 753-3447   1-877-733-7320